D0282433

The Peabody Ducks

created by Jean J. Garbarini

written by Martha L. Garrety

illustrated by Phyllis Baily

published by

Darla G. Sellers   Vicki G. Bennett

The Peabody Ducks
P.O. Box 130777
Birmingham, Alabama 35213-0777

The Peabody Ducks
P.O. 240543
Memphis, Tennessee 38124-0543

First Printing	1982
Second Printing	1983
Third Printing	1984
Fourth Printing	1986
Fifth Printing	1989
Sixth Printing	1994

DELTA GRAPHICS

Memphis, Tennessee
(901) 372-1565

This book

is

dedicated to our children

and

grandchildren

and

to children of all ages.

PREFACE

Most once upon a time tales

Are stories stretched quite tall,

Or are of just-pretend things

That never were at all.

But there is one about some special ducks

That's absolutely true,

And in the pages of this book

It is written just for you.

If you think seeing is believing,

There is a place where you can see—

At the famous Peabody Hotel

In Memphis, Tennessee!

Once upon a time a family of ordinary ducks
swam in a pond on Mr. Pembroke's farm.

One day Mr. Pembroke told them that they were all moving to a big city. "To the city? What a pity! Here on the farm it's so peaceful and pretty!" quacked the ducks.

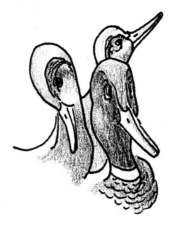

Three little sad birds of a feather

Huddled ever so closely together

Then flapped their wings in rage

As Mr. Pembroke put them in a travel cage.

"Cheer up!" Mr. Pembroke said to each duck
And away they went in his big red truck.

Soon they were on an adventuresome trip
Crossing the mighty 'Mississip'.

The fact that the bridge looked like a big M
Did not mean a single thing to them.

But as the sky was turning dark
They saw the lights of Mud Island Park.

"Must be Memphis," one of them said,

Then under his wing he tucked his head
And wished he was home in his own little bed.

Now the surprise Mr. Pembroke saved to tell
Was their new home would be the Peabody Hotel.

Even more incredible, but it is no spoof —
They would sleep in a penthouse on the hotel roof.

Mr. Pembroke would stay and be their guide
On the daily elevator ride.
Down,
down,
down to the lobby floor
Where a red carpet is rolled to the elevator door.
When the door opens and the ducks appear . . .

An announcer says, ''The ducks are here!''
The waiting crowds clap and cheer

22

As a Sousa March plays loud and clear.

The ducks march on the carpet to the lobby pool
Filled with Memphis water that is clear and cool,
Crowned with flowers colorful and pretty
Again and forever in the heart of the city.

Here for a few hours every day
They swim and eat and splash and play.
In the Peabody lobby the visitors swarm
To watch the mallard ducks perform.
Now when they see these people smile
They are glad they came to stay for awhile.

Then back on the rooftop and just before sleep
One little duck is heard to peep,
"Thank you, Lord, for my good luck
And for letting me be a Peabody duck!"

The ducks referred to in this book are just one group
of a long line of ducks that have entertained at the
Peabody Hotel for many years.
Your parents or grandparents may already have seen
or heard of them.
Eventually, the ducks all return to the farm
allowing other ducks to take a turn.
So, the happiest thought of these fine feathered friends
Is that theirs may be a story that never ends.
Now if you have not seen them, please don't fret,
You and your grandchildren may get there yet.